Love &
Happiness

A collection of personal reflections and quotes

Yasmin Mogahed

Visit my website at:
www.yasminmogahed.com
or
www.facebook.com/ymogahed

Cover & Book Design: Peter Gould | www.peter-gould.com
Book Layout: Megan McCullough

ISBN: 978-0-9985373-7-5
First Edition

Published in the United States of America

Introduction

Things fall apart. And they break sometimes. Like many of you, my
journey hasn't always been easy. Pain is very real. And so is loss.
Sometimes it's hard not to let the weight of what we carry—or the
memory of what we've lost—take over. Many of us know the reality
of struggle, and so many people suffer in silence. It's hard. It's
hard not to give up when we face the repeated disappointments
of life. Like some of you, I've known loneliness. I've known defeat.
I've fallen many times chasing mirages, and broken many bones
making castles in life's fading sands. Sometimes, all it took was one
solid wave to destroy what I had spent years building.

So I decided to give it a voice. All of it: the tears, the pain. And the lessons. The things I saw and learned and gained along my life path needed a voice. I wanted to give back, in hopes of helping myself and others survive. But then it wasn't just about surviving. I didn't just want people to survive inside their storms. I wanted people to thrive inside their storms.

And so I wrote, as I walked through my own.

The words found in this book became my voice and my letter to the world. They became my deepest attempt to, not just pick myself up, but others along the way. I wrote because, just as we will fall in life, so will we rise. That's the thing about this world. It never gives us only one kind of path. There is pain. Yes. And loss. And even darkness. But there is also light. There is hope. There is beauty.

And there is also love and happiness.

Yasmin Mogahed

There are many pieces that make up our lives:
Moments that break us. Moments that raise and shape
us. Decisions we make to hold on. Or let go. People who
enter our lives and leave us changed forever. The ones we
love, the ones that hurt us, or heal us, or leave us.

Sometimes we don't understand these pieces—or even
despair over them. It's only when time goes by and we
look back, that we suddenly can see our whole life like a
perfectly designed puzzle.

Don't be afraid of the puzzle piece you're in now. It will
fit perfectly… just like the rest. How could it not?
The Designer is perfect.

Your greatest tragedy is that you actually find comfort in your tragedy. Because it's familiar. The pain is safe.

Love, joy, and vulnerability aren't safe. Because they can be lost.

So you choose the 'safety' of your prison, over the risk of your happiness. You choose this because it's all you've ever known. To you, even pain is better than numbness. So you find safety in it. This is the definition of self-harm. To cut, just to feel. Because you say feeling something is better than feeling nothing at all.

Stop the self-harm. If God hands you a gift and you take it, but don't say thank you, we call that ingratitude. But if God hands you a gift and you refuse to even take it—that is the greatest ingratitude.

Beware of complete focus and dependence on deeds. If they're good, focusing on them will make you arrogant. If they're bad, focusing on their 'greatness' will make you despair, and focusing on their 'smallness' will make you transgress.

Focus instead on God. Seeing His right over you will never allow you to be arrogant about a good deed. Seeing His mercy over you will never allow you to despair at a sin. And seeing His Greatness over you will never allow you to belittle a sin.

*D*on't *worry.*

The help of God comes in proportion to the hardship.

The greater your pain, the sweeter the comfort.

The harder your test, the larger the reward.

The bigger your wound, the stronger the healing.

The deeper the hole carves into you,
the more fill you can contain.

I can't remember when I came here.

And I don't see when I'll leave.

But I know this: I only came to leave.

You wondered why He created the void.

You couldn't understand why the emptiness existed.

Then you realized that a full person doesn't ask.

The one who feels 'rich' doesn't beg.

If your heart is broken, know that He is Al Jabbar,
the One who mends.

If your heart is dead, know that the One who can give
life to the dead body, can give life to your dead heart.

Don't think being *religious* means
becoming harsh or hard.

When Allah's love enters a heart,
it is softened—not hardened.

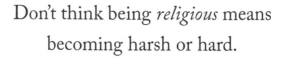

To all those suffering from sadness or depression, know that it isn't because you're weak. It isn't because you're just not grateful enough. It isn't because you're just not religious enough. It isn't because you don't have enough faith. It isn't because God is angry with you. To all the well-meaning people who tell you this, just smile. And know deep in your heart that the tests of God come in different forms to different people. And know that, by the help of God, every test can become a tool to get closer to Him. And that, verily, with hardship comes ease—and like all things of this world—this too shall pass.

Many broken people approach me for help. Because I am one of them. I suppose healing has become a lifestyle for me. But I guess you never really become an expert at pain. One thing I have learned is this: Don't control the tears. They are there for a reason. They were sent to heal you. Cry, because that's how we heal. Especially cry to Allah. I know that is the only reason I still walk around.

Cry especially at tahajjud.

I can give no better advice to the broken.

I can give no better advice to myself.

The mind replays what the heart can't delete.
The heart remembers, even when the mind forgets.

For those who wish to turn their lives around, it begins by focusing on and perfecting the salah. Once you put salah back as the priority—before school, work, fun, socializing, shopping, TV, ball games—only then can you turn your life around.

The irony of this truth is that many people are deceived into thinking that they need to first turn their life around, before they can start praying. This thinking is a dangerous trick of shaytan, who knows that it is salah itself which will provide the fuel and guidance necessary to turn our life around. It is like a driver whose car is on empty, but insists on finishing the journey before filling up on gas. That person won't be going anywhere. And in the same way, such people end up in the same place for years: Not praying, and not changing their lives.

Shaytan challenged them, and won.

In so doing, we have allowed him to steal from us what is priceless. Our homes and our cars are so precious to us, that we would never think to leave them unprotected. So we pay hundreds of dollars on security systems to keep them safe. And yet our hearts are left unprotected, to be stolen by the worst of thieves—a thief who has vowed God Himself to be our relentless enemy till the end of time. A thief who is not simply stealing some carved metal with a Mercedes symbol on it. A thief who is stealing our eternal soul and everlasting ticket to Paradise.

When you're going through a hard time, it's easy to become consumed by the moment.

Don't let yourself get stuck.

Focus your mind and heart on a time of peace before the hardship began. Remind yourself that you existed before it—and you will continue to exist after it passes away.

When talking about marriage, Allah says your spouses are garments for you. A garment may or may not fit perfectly—but either way, it covers imperfections, protects, and beautifies.

Peace doesn't exist outside. It can only exist inside.

And the peace that is on the inside cannot be taken away by anyone. No matter what they do. No matter what they say. No matter what they threaten.

If your paradise is in your heart, no one can take it from you.

Love without dependency. Love is about giving.
Dependency is about taking.

Suffering is the place before acceptance, buried
deep in the land of uncertainty and false hope.
I found peace in acceptance.

I found peace in letting go.

∽

Don't think of the trials in your life (balaa) as just a 'test' in the human form. Allah is not like a professor who hands you a test, moves away, and just watches from afar to see how you'll do. Allah is our murabee— the One who raises us with more mercy than a mother raises a child.

The Prophet ﷺ tells us that when Allah wills good for someone, He sends them balaa (trials or tests). When Allah wills good for us, He purifies us. That is why each person is tested in what they love most. In other words, our greatest possible 'competitor' in our love for God is what may be withheld or sacrificed. This is the purification process because it cures the heart of competitors.

Why was Prophet Ibrahim (AS) asked to slaughter the most beloved thing to him? Did Allah actually want him to kill his son? No. He didn't kill his son. He killed the attachment. By being willing to sacrifice what he loved most, he had slaughtered any possible competing love. Allah was raising him, purifying him, and elevating him. Allah tells us, "By no means shall you attain righteousness unless you give (freely) of that which you love." (3:92)

One of the best tests for love is remembrance.

You can't forget what you love, and you can hardly remember what you don't.

The more you love God, the more you remember. And the more you remember, the more you love.

Be fully human.

Why is it that we refuse to accept the full human experience—the full design of the human experiment? We want the happiness, without the sadness. The light, without the dark. The ease, without the hardship. When a child learns to walk, the falls are part of the process. But we want to learn to walk, without struggling through the falls. The fall is just as important as the rise. The slip of Adam was a lesson, not an oversight of God. God gives us the strength and the weakness. Not as an oversight, not as a flaw in the design. He gives us both because each part plays a purpose in our development, and our ultimate success.

Don't stunt the process of your growth by trying to limit the spectrum of the human plan. Many of us fear failure so much, that we are afraid to try. But reflect on this: Was it through your successes or through your failures that you learned your deepest lessons? Our successes encourage us. But it is our failures that teach us. In life, we need both. Success gives us the motivation to keep going, while failure teaches us the difficult, often painful, yet necessary, lessons we need to grow and fulfill our ultimate purpose.

Sometimes you search so hard for words.

You look for a way to interpret the language of your heart and the unspoken universe you feel.

But in the end you are left with nothing but silence. And deep down you hope it's understood.

Sometimes when we are hurting ourselves and not able to stop, Allah, out of His infinite mercy, takes the source of hurt away from us.

But we are a lot like children playing with a knife. We don't care that the knife is cutting us, and could even kill us.

So we cry when it's taken away.

In our own futile quest for human perfection,
we miss the whole point: God's perfection.

If you wonder how you'll get through this new heartbreak, just think back.

Remember all you've been through in the past. And how each time you swore you'd never get through it. But you did. And look where you're at now.

This too shall pass!

The cause of jealousy and ingratitude is that with regards to ourselves, we see only our trials—but not our blessings. But with regards to others, we see only their blessings—but not their trials.

As much as you can, keep dunya (worldly life) in your hand—not in your heart.

That means when someone insults you, keep it out of your heart so it doesn't make you bitter or defensive. When someone praises you, also keep it out of your heart, so it doesn't make you arrogant and self-deluded. When you face hardship and stress, don't absorb it in your heart, so you don't become hopeless and overwhelmed. Instead, keep it in your hands and realize that everything passes.

When you're given a gift by God, don't hold it in your heart. Hold it in your hand so that you don't begin to love the gift more than the giver. And so that when it is taken away you can truly respond with 'inna lillahi wa inna ilayhi rajioon': 'indeed we belong to God, and to God we return'.

Pain, joy, and even loss will all pass away.

What remains is only what they do to us.

∾

Sometimes we lose hope in turning to God and asking for His help because we feel like we have done too much wrong.

And yet think of a child who has just angered his mother and immediately after, trips and falls on the stairs. Even if that child had just angered his mother to tears, the moment he falls and cries for help, she runs to him. This is human mercy. And God is infinitely more merciful than a mother is to her child.

So, do you think—no matter what you've done— when you're falling and cry out to the *most* merciful... He wouldn't come save you?

I love the people of the shrapnel. The ones who got struck so deeply, that a piece always remains.

They have healed, but they walk around with a constant reminder of their poverty and their need for the Doctor. So they live their lives in constant nearness to His door, always desperate for His care and protection. Ever aware of their poverty and need.

These are the weak, who've been made powerful. Their poverty has made them rich.

Dive into the center of your pain. Find the jewel. If you hit anger, you're not there yet. Dig deeper. You need to keep going. Past the anger. Past the bitterness. You will need to swim deeper. You will know when you've arrived.

You will know… once you reach compassion.

Why does God give us pain? Why did all the Prophets suffer great loss and trial? Purification? Yes, of course pain purifies. But the Prophets were sinless.

Perhaps it is our own trials, our own losses, and pain, that carve within our soul a deeper capacity to feel and show mercy, compassion and empathy to others.

Perhaps the purpose of our own brokenness is to build a greater capacity to serve the broken and the wounded.

Perhaps we were put on this earth only to serve. Serve God, through service to people. And maybe everything we've experienced in life is meant to aid in this purpose. Maybe our trials were meant to carve out the compassion, the empathy and the mercy. And our blessings and gifts were meant to provide the tools and the strength needed to aid others.

Let the beauty of what you seek, transform what you are.
Let the beauty of what you are, transform what you do.

We get so scared sometimes. Afraid of all that can go wrong. All that can be lost. But in our debilitating fear, we lose focus. We see the sickness, but not the cure. The storm, but not the shelter. Yes, there are armies and Red Seas. Yes, there are flames. But remember, the sickness, the storm, the fire, the armies and the Sea, are all creations in the hands of the Sovereign.

He saved Ayyoub (AS) from the sickness, Nuh (AS) from the storm, Ibrahim (AS) from the flames, and Musa (AS) from the armies and the Sea. It wasn't that they didn't face these hardships. They did. They were surrounded by them. But Allah kept them safe, even while in the belly of the calamity.

Our focus is wrong. We fear the storm, because we don't see the Shelter. We fear the Red Sea, because we don't see the One who can split it in two. It is not the storm we should fear...
but the distance from Shelter.

You spent your life looking for love.

But one day you will realize that it was in those moments of giving—not in receiving—that you found happiness.

Often what makes us fall into despair is focusing on the wrong things.

For example, if we've sinned, we focus on the sin, rather than the Most Merciful. If we're broken, we focus on the break, instead of Al Jabbar, the One who mends. If we're in pain, we focus on the pain itself, instead of the One who removes all pain. If we are wounded, we focus on the wound, instead of the One who heals all wounds. If we're scared, we focus on the fear, instead of the Protector. And if we're facing a problem, we see the problem, but not the One who can solve it. We see the lion, but not the lion tamer. We see the imperfections of dunya, but not the perfection of Allah. We see the immediate, but not the Tomorrow; the tree, but not the fruit; the thorn, but not the rose. All our pain, all our despair, all our hopelessness, stems from looking at the creation, instead of the Creator.

Ask yourself: What is your heart looking at?

There are internal chains and external chains.

All the external chains in the world won't enslave you, if you are free inside.

And all the external 'freedom' in the world won't liberate you, if you are chained inside.

Take the people out of the equation.

It's not about them.
It's not about how they feel about you or treat you.

It's about you.
Your own principles, your own character.

Treat the people without seeing the people.
Treat the people while seeing Allah.

Don't ever resent the people who've left you or hurt you or let you down. They're all part of your story.

Widen the lens. Don't get caught up in moments. Happy or sad, they all pass. And what remains is only the heart inside your chest—free or shackled, beautiful or ugly.

Don't worry about what the people say.

Sometimes they'll praise you. Sometimes they'll condemn you.

All these things fade away.

And in the end, Allah takes care of everything. Perfectly.

Fasting is so beautiful. The fasting person is saying: "Dear God, I love food. I love drink. I love to fulfill my desires. But I love You more. And so I will give up what I love—even what I need—for Your sake."

Know that this sacrifice is not taken lightly by Allah. That's why He rewards for fasting as He rewards for nothing else, and you are given two happinesses: In this life, when you break your fast, and in the next, when you meet Him.

He withheld what you love,
to teach you about the nature of this life.

Then He gave you what you love,
to teach you about the nature of the next.

People think that tests only come in the form of hardships. God also tests us with ease. And it's often in the test of ease that we fail most.

God gave you money, status, beauty, intellect, health. Are you using those things as He wants or as you want?

He made you beautiful. Are you covering it?
He made you intelligent, are you arrogant?
He made you rich, are you generous?
He surrounded you with gifts. Are you grateful?

Are you depending on the money, the status, the people, your own self—or on Him?

I think we all carry within us many different versions of ourselves.

Our true, greatest, and most honest version of ourselves can either be developed and nourished, or it can remain dead from neglect.

Most people opt for the easiest version, rather than the best. But in the end, which version lives, which version thrives, and which version dies, depends on the choices we make, and the people in our lives.

Don't think for a moment that your heart is 'strong'.

The heart is a vulnerable fool. It turns more easily than you turn your head. That's why it's called 'qalb' (that which turns).

Protect it with layer upon layer of guards. And the only guard is the *consistent* remembrance of God.

To all those who have ever lost someone or something they love: What you think you've lost, is not lost.

Open up the barrier you have created inside your heart between this life and the next. They are two rooms in the same house. What you love is just in the next room. And you are walking towards that room.

The recipe for misery is simple: Carry a deep sense of entitlement and expectations. And every time you give, keep track of what you are 'owed'.

The recipe for happiness is also simple: Give out of love—not entitlement or expectations.

We spend so much time asking God
to cure us of our hardships.

But we never stop to consider that
our hardships are curing us.

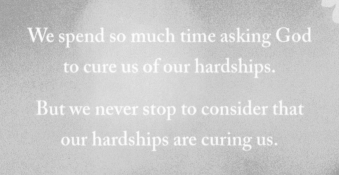

There's an amazing thing about broken hearts.

When you don't get what you want, you discover a need. When you discover a need, you begin to ask. When a request is unfulfilled, you keep asking.

Sometimes He doesn't give you what you ask for when He wants to give you something more. Sometimes He doesn't give to us right away because He knows there's something better. Or so we can keep asking.

Because it is in the process of begging that we are elevated and brought nearer. It is in the process of asking that we are brought to the foot of His thrown. It is your need and helplessness that drove you to His thrown. He deprives to give.

It was in those moments of loneliness that I found You.

Adam (AS) ate from a forbidden tree. Iblis refused to bow. But what distinguished them from each other, was their response *after* they slipped.

The mark of character is not in whether or not we make mistakes. Everyone makes mistakes. The true mark of character is in how we respond *after* we've made a mistake.

How intensely you cling to things, is dependent on your internal and external state.

A starving person clings to any sign of food. A prisoner sees any bond as not just an object of love, but a refuge.

To loosen the clinging and obsessive nature of the attachment, you must change the state. Be not starving or imprisoned. Feed and free the heart, and you will cure the attachment. There's no other cure.

Hardships are intended to soften us—not harden us.
If we find that hardships are making us harder inside,
it is a sign that we are depending on ourselves
instead of Allah.

Yesterday, the trees surrounding me were bare. Today they're covered with blossoms! Subhann al khaliq!

He shows us seasons on the earth to help us understand the seasons of our heart! He shows us His power to give and take life.

If you thought your heart was dead, remember that the One who gives life to the dead land can give life to the dead hearts! And once He resurrects your heart, He can remake it completely. More beautiful than it ever was! Allahu Akbar!

I have been through some dark times in my life and I have had to make some very hard decisions. But I'll tell you what I've learned...

Life isn't supposed to be miserable. It isn't supposed to be excruciatingly painful. It isn't supposed to suffocate or drain you.

Are there parts of life that will make you feel this way? Yes. Absolutely. But, why? We must ask why. Why do we go through these things? Is it so that we stay still and bear it stoically? Is it to passively endure and call it "sabr" or patience?

Absolutely not.

In fact we go through misery, pain, suffocation for the exact opposite reason: To push us towards change. Movement. Growth. "Sabr" is not standing still. "Sabr" is not being passive. Sabr is the endurance necessary to make the change needed to move one step closer to where Allah wants us to be.

God created pain, in both the physical and spiritual world, as a wakeup call. As a motivator and accelerator towards action, movement, and change to alleviate the pain.

When a person has an infection, they feel fever. When a person's heart is clogged, they experience chest pain, or heart attack. A person can ignore fever or chest pain and call it "patience" or "sabr". But if this pain is ignored and just numbed long enough, the sickness only increases. Until it actually kills us. Pain is a warning. A smoke alarm for the sleeping soul.

If you feel suffocated, it's probably because you're not getting enough oxygen. It works the same spiritually and emotionally, as it does physically.

Be brave enough to dig deep, to be honest. And then to take the action and change necessary to save your life.

But, be careful. Never, ever take this action alone. Seek strength and guidance in God. Only then will you never drown or get lost.

Internal freedom requires external struggle.
And external freedom requires internal struggle.

Beauty is the goal. Beauty of the heart.

Judge every experience in life as either good or bad,
not based on how much pleasure or pain it brought,
but based on how beautiful or ugly it made your heart.

The best way to let go of bitterness is to stop seeing the creation, and only see the Creator. Whatever has befallen you, was not meant to pass you. Whatever has passed you, was not meant to befall you. And everything that came or did not come can be used to bring you close to Him. This means it was all good for you. That is the power of faith. The Prophet ﷺ said, "The matter of a believer is strange. Everything is good for him."

Some hearts hear each other—even in silence.
Sometimes what's separated in this life
is joined in the next.

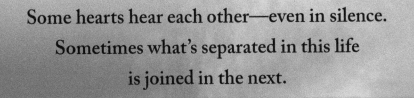

Sometimes the more one grows in religious practice, the more they grow in self-righteousness and judgment.

This is a sign of a problem inside. It is a sign that internal cleaning is necessary.

Growing in religion should make us grow in compassion—not judgment. The heart filled with God is softened, not hardened. If the heart is becoming harsh or hardened towards people, perhaps it is not God filling the heart. Perhaps it is the self, decorated by the false cloak of piety and religious devotion.

When the Creator is the only thing you *need*,

there is a sweetness in loving the creation.

No longer a hunger and pain.

When they slept, He was awake. When they broke, He held you up. When every means failed, He saved you. When all the creation left you, He remained. He always remains. Never forget when the storms pushed you to your knees and there was no one else who could help you, He carried you. When you were broken and you swore this time it couldn't be fixed, never forget who fixed it. Never forget what He saved you from. Never forget how He put you back together. That moment when you felt helpless and alone, never forget who never left. To forget this is the greatest heedlessness. No matter who or what may be beside you now, never forget those moments when it was only Him. Only Him. That is loyalty.

Try not to confuse 'attachment' with 'love'.

Attachment is about fear and dependency, and has more to do with love of self than love of another.

Love without attachment is the purest love because it isn't about what others can give you because you are empty. It is about what you can give others because you are already full.

Allah is Al Wahab (the one who loves to give gifts) and Al Kareem (the most generous). Therefore, the default is that He loves to give.

So, think about it.

We must know that if Al Wahab and Al Kareem has withheld something from us, it must be because Al Aleem (the most knowing) and Al Hakeem (the most wise) knows in His knowledge and wisdom that at this time it is best for us that it be withheld. And so, Al Rahman (the most merciful) withholds. Know that He withholds to give.

We don't forgive to free others.
We forgive to free ourselves.

Don't let your sorrows drown you. Use them to deepen you, humble and soften you. Use them to build your empathy and compassion for the world.

Your sorrow was never meant to overtake you; like everything else in life, it is only a tool. To beautify and strengthen you.

Every moment is its own universe. Each moment brings with it a new birth, a new opportunity to live, to turn back, to renew. Each moment is a new chance to get it right.

And with each moment is also a death. Let the past die. If you messed up yesterday, that universe is already dead and gone. Right now is your new reality. Capture it, before it dies.

See through the test of wealth.

The money you were given belongs to God. Not you.

It was given *through* you, not *to* you.
It was given to be given. Not kept.

There is a very deep difference between healthy remorse and shame. Healthy remorse is a motivator in the path to God; shame is a barrier to God, and a tool of Shaytan.

How do you know the difference? If your 'guilt' motivates you to get closer to Allah, it's from God and it's healthy. If your 'guilt' makes you feel so bad about yourself that you give up or stop trying, it's not from Allah! It's from Shaytan. Don't be fooled. Self-hatred isn't divine. It's satanic.

Learn to have enough self-compassion to accept your humanness. Learn to put your hope in Allah—not in your deeds. And learn to acknowledge your faults, but never let them define or consume you. Or paralyze you. Learn to get back up when you stumble. Because stumbling is part of the Divine plan… to bring us all back to Him.

Learn to let go of what isn't meant to be.

Realize that nothing lasts forever. Not even broken hearts.

Know that the night is given to you so you can recognize the light that follows. That always follows.

Rejoice! Rejoice in the knowledge that Allah often takes things that you love away… in order to replace them with something better!

Don't despair if your heart has been through a lot of trauma. Sometimes that's how beautiful hearts are remade: They are shattered first.

To some, a Monet is only a collection of dots. To others, it is a perfect masterpiece.

To some, Islam is nothing but a code of rules and regulations. But, to those who understand, it is a perfect vision of life.

There are some people who could hear you speak a
thousand words and still not understand you.

And there are others who will understand—
without you even speaking a word.

I think one of the reasons we are so afraid to admit our mistakes and weaknesses is because we believe our weaknesses make us less worthy of love and respect.

The truth is, they don't. Our mistakes make us human. Our admitting them, makes us beautiful.

Sabr is internal quiet in the midst of external noise. It is the internal refuge within the external storm.

Sabr is to see through illusions, to resist, to act—even when it's hard. To keep going—even when it hurts.

Showing vulnerability isn't a weakness. It's a strength. Keep the heart soft. Be unafraid of the creation. Be real with Allah, yourself, and others. And give. Give out of compassion, knowing that we're all vulnerable. We're all struggling. We're all poor. And only He is rich. There's so much beauty in that poverty. See the beauty in your poverty, because Your Provider is rich. Your Protector is strong. There's pain in this world. But there's also so much beauty.

Let the pain prepare you for the beauty.

I loved. I lost. So I learned to love what is never lost.

Then what I loved that can be lost was through what cannot be lost… so it was never lost.

We live in a world that teaches us to deny our emotions. That to feel is to be weak.

But by doing this, we not only deny our nature and a creation of God, we deny the very means of reaching Him.

How can we reach God without love, fear, regret, hope? How can we reach God without the heart?

Like every other creation of God, our emotions, our desires, our needs are put in us for a reason.

Use them—but never let them use you. Control them. Never allow them to control you.

Don't worry if your heart hurts today.

Hearts change every day.

And He is the turner of hearts.

Your hardships and disappointments are your emptying. If you leave it there, you remain empty and only achieve the first half of Al Kalima: 'La Illaha'.

Your thikr (remembrance) is your filling, and the completion of Al Kalima: 'illa Allah'.

We often wonder why God gives and takes, constricts, and expands. What we forget is that human beings understand things by their opposites.

Without dark, we can't understand light. Without hardship, we wouldn't *experience* ease. Without the existence of deprivation and loss, we couldn't grasp the need for gratitude or the virtue of patience. And without separation, we wouldn't taste the sweetness of reunion.

Glory be to the One who gives—even when He takes.

Musa (as) had a speech impediment and was cast out for accidentally killing a man.

Yusuf (as) was thrown into a well by his own brothers and became a slave.

Ibrahim (as) was thrown into fire.

But Allah made Musa (as) split the Sea and defeat the superpower and his army, made Yusuf (as) become the king, and made Ibrahim (as) an ummah of himself and the father of the prophets.

Allah's promise is true and His help is near.

But it requires a process. A process that you cannot speed up or ignore. A process that begins with complete reliance (tawwakul) and is sustained by the water of tawheed.

Purify your heart. Then follow it.

There are some people who enter your life like gems. These are the real diamonds. They have no ulterior motives, no inferiority complex, no superiority complex, no need to prove that they are better than you, or seek to have more than you. They don't feel entitled and aren't needy or dependent. They are not superficial or fake. They remind you of God and they understand you, when no other person does. They don't wear a mask with you or pretend to be perfect. They are just real with you and honestly and sincerely only want good for you. You feel you can tell them anything without worrying that they will judge you or put you down for being imperfect. They know your flaws, but love you anyway. And they are loyal. You know they'll be there for you. They'll always have your back. And best of all, time and distance doesn't change this.

If you've met even one person in your entire life like this, you're blessed.

Rejoice. Rejoice in the knowledge that the One whom you have entrusted has split the Sea and cooled the fire to save His slave. Can He not then save you, even when you see no way out?

Rejoice in the knowledge that in Him nothing is ever lost. Rejoice because His promise has already come to pass. And He has promised you His help. He promised you everything you love and want. In Him, hope is never dead. In Him, love is never lost. He is the Ever Living, the Source of Love. How can you fear loss when in His hands are the keys to all things?

Seek everything you want through Him, rejoice in Him, hope in Him, turn to Him, and nothing will ever be lost or dead.

When you're in pain, don't focus on the pain. Focus on the One who heals all pain.

When you're stuck, don't look at the Red Sea in front of you. Look at the One who can split it in two!

The heart is a confusing, altering thing.

No state is forever. No state of bliss lasts forever.
But no state of pain does, either. They all pass.

So if you experience happiness, ask Allah to make
it forever in jennah. And if you experience sadness,
ask Allah to make it a means of purification and
elevation for you.

And know that this too shall pass.

Empowerment comes when we stop being victims
and become students of our lives.

We must study every experience and how to
use it to learn, grow.

And then overcome.

When the pain overtakes you, reach inside. Gather the broken pieces, and hand them to God. Ask Him to remake your heart. Different, this time. Stronger. More beautiful. This is how we are made, and remade by the Maker.

He gives you a glimpse, but doesn't allow you to mistaken it for the Real thing.

So He gives you the beauty, but doesn't allow it to last. He gives you love, but makes it hurt sometimes. He gives you the most beautifully colored leaves, but soon makes them dry up and fall to the ground.

He allows you to glimpse—even touch—the Kaaba, but makes you have to leave even that behind. He gave you His messenger , but even he had to die.

All this to teach us this one lesson: "If you worshipped Mohammed, know that Mohammed is dead. But if you worship Allah, know that He never dies." If you worshipped this life—its beauty, love, leaves, people—know that this life and *everything* in it will die. But if you worship Allah, know that He never dies.

Your life is nothing more than a love story.

Between you and God. Nothing more.

Every person, every experience, every gift, every loss, every pain is sent to your path for one reason and one reason only: To bring you back to Him.

My failures taught me what my 'successes' never could.

It's going to keep hurting, until you realize that there are places in the human heart created by, and for, God alone.

True beauty grows with age.
The more you grow, the more love you can contain.

With time, you begin to know yourself; and in that
knowledge, you finally discover what you actually
want. What you've always needed. No book can teach
you that. Only life can.

When you're in need, in pain, or confused, don't speak. Listen. Listen for the duaa He inspires in your heart. And then ask. Beg. And don't stop begging.

∾

We often wonder why those we love most also cause us the most pain. The reason is that anything other than God (our children, our spouses, our money, our jobs, our desires) that we place at the center of our existence *will* be the cause of our greatest pain.

The heart was created by and for God. The heart was created to know and love God. The heart was created to be given to God. To be filled with God.

The heart that is given to or filled by any other thing, suffers the most painful impoverishment and death.

Never base your relationships with the creation (people, money, career) on being filled. Base your relationships with the creation on giving. Leave your 'filling' to God.

I tell you to keep going, not because it's easy.
Not because it doesn't hurt.

I tell you to keep going because there's no other
way. To stop is to die. Life is in motion. In growth.
In change. Life is in seeking and in finding. Life
is in redemption. Each moment is a new birth. A
new chance to come back, to get it right.

A new chance to make it better.

Run towards the creation, you lose God and the creation. Run towards God, you gain God *and* the creation.

Allah is Al Wadud (The Source of Love). Therefore, love comes from God—not people. As one author, Charles F. Haanel, writes: "To acquire love… fill yourself up with it until you become a magnet."

When you fill yourself with the Source of love (Al Wadud), you become a magnet for love.

He created both night and day.

If it's dark in your life right now, be patient.
The sun always rises.

And if it's light right now, be thankful. But don't get
attached to the sun. It is in its design to also set.

Praise Him for both the night and the day and know
that He never sets.

Seek those with expanded hearts.

The capacity not only to cope, but the capacity to feel. To feel every range of emotion. The ones who welcome all the seasons of their heart. The ones who live *through* life. Not around or below it. Through the fog, the rain, the waves. And the storm.

Because that's just it. You can't get to the other side. You can't get to the sun—unless you forge through the storm. You can't arrive home, if you shut off your engine once the rain comes.

You *must* feel it to get over it. There's no other way.

But I promise you this: It will be worth it in the end.

So worth it.

The sun is warm, dear heart. The sun is warm. And it will heal you and mend what was broken.

This process is temporary.

But like all things in life, you *must* be true to it. You must be true to every portion of the process.

You must take what is given by the Doctor, even if today's medicine is bitter. You must taste it.

And know that tomorrow's dose will be sweet.

Trust the process. He knows. He knows what He's doing. He knows your heart. He knows your pain. He knows what you desire. He is not far. He hears. And He doesn't forget. He never forgets. He knows what you need. And when you need it.

He is here. He is near.

Trust the process. Trust the process and take today's medicine—whatever it may be.

The Doctor knows. Trust me. He knows. And He loves. More than you can imagine. More than your mother ever could. Never lose faith. Or hope.

You can't see it now. But He isn't breaking your ship. He's building it. It will make sense soon. Be patient and beg for ease.

Not even strength. Just ease.

And it will come. Your opening will come.

It will come.

Ya Fattah. Ya Kareem.

Things are most often not as they seem.

What looks peaceful outside, is often total chaos inside. And what looks like chaos outside, is often peaceful inside.

So don't ever judge. Don't envy what looks perfect and don't despair at what looks broken.

Others don't hear it and they'll call me crazy, but I hear peace in the sunset, and feel no loneliness in the forest.

The trees all speak to those who listen. They scream submission and strength all at once. When commanded to stand, they stand tall. Nothing can shake them. When commanded to bow down, they bow, broken, but not dead. Humble strength. When told to die, they die. They die orange, red and yellow. Even their death is beautiful. So beautiful. I want to die like them, giving color to the world as I leave. Because we all leave. Every moment we are leaving.

The question is not whether we leave; the question is how we leave. When the tree is called back, it rises again. Reborn

When we see people around the world whose bodies are starving to death, we should feel mercy and concern.

But why don't we feel the same pain and concern when we see people whose hearts and souls are starving to death?

Ironically, we worry more about the death of the body, when it is the body that disintegrates, while the soul remains.

Allah withholds a portion of what is desired to keep you needy, to keep you at His door. To keep an empty place in your heart. That only He can fill. The slave keeps begging for what is desired, not knowing that His Lord is preparing for him what is greater.

And then when Allah gives, there are different types of currencies. And they are not equal. There are lesser currencies and greater, more valuable currencies. Some people are paid their recompense in dunya currency. And this is from among the favors of Allah. But there are others who are paid in a different currency: The currency of Divine nearness.

The one who is paid in *that* currency can never be satisfied with only the lesser currency again.

May Allah, the Most Generous, bless us with both currencies.

When you're real, God surrounds you with real.

And nothing less. That's why He will remove people from your life, sometimes.

That's why He will close doors.
That's why He will put up inpenetratable walls.

Don't ever think it's to deprive you.

It isn't.

By focusing on our negative emotions, we enlarge them. And then we drown in them. A negative state is like wearing dark glasses. They make everything we see look different than it really is.

But don't be deceived. Nothing is actually dark. It's just that temporary lens which is making it appear so.

The secret is to understand that what you're seeing right now isn't real. And it's temporary. Don't give up because it's dark. Tomorrow your lens will change.

And then so will your world.

Only when our internal state is not
dependent on our external situation
will our external situation change,
and will we find real, lasting peace.

Beware of viewing your relationship with God as a transactional one.

Thinking He's just repaying you for your works, creates a dangerous sense of entitlement when you see your works as good. But, the subtle danger lies in what happens when you see your works as bad.

You lose all hope.

God to you becomes like a drill sergeant (God forbid), ready to withhold and punish, instead of the One more merciful than a mother to her child, ready to forgive, forbear and give—although you have done nothing to deserve it and cannot repay it in any way.

Every time I got to a drop of water,
I mistaken it for the ocean.
And then God would teach me.
So I kept walking.
I came across a larger drop.
I mistaken it for the ocean.
Again.
And again He taught me.
To keep going.
Don't stop.
And don't give up.
Keep going.
It's about trust, dear soul.
Trust. And patience.
Not the still kind.
The kind that keeps walking,
Through the storm.
Through the illusion.
Through the mirage.
Through every false door,
And imaginary shelter.
It's not easy to fall on your face.
But it's even harder to get back up.
And not just get back up...

Get back up and keep hoping.
That's hard.
That requires the deepest level of
  reliance.
And hope.
Beautiful hope.
Bulletproof hope.
Irrational optimism.
Nothing short of it.
Keep going.
Dear beautiful soul,
You almost drowned in drops...
looking for the Sea.
Dear soul, He didn't let you drown.
You kept going.
Even when you had to crawl.
In the rain.
In the pitch black night.
You kept going.
And He is leading you, dear soul.
He is leading you, dear soul.
He is leading you...
...to the Sea.
Allah kareem.

I have nothing but Your generosity to put my hope in. Nothing. For I stand at Your door holding broken scraps… and yet you open. Save me from this storm. I am the most helpless of all your slaves. And I am lost. Wandering in the middle of a forest trying to find my way. But all the trees look the same, and each path just leads back to the beginning. No one finds their way out of this forest—except whom You save. Save me. For truly, truly I cannot save myself.

The emptiness will overtake you until you realize that your salvation lies in thankfulness.

When I cry or lose or bruise, so long as I am still alive, nothing is ultimate.

So long as there is still a tomorrow, a next moment, there is hope, there is change, there is redemption.

What is lost, is not lost forever.

When we think we're perfect,
we expect perfection from others.

When we start to recognize our own weaknesses,
we begin to be more forgiving of the weaknesses in others.

But, this dark place is not the end.

Remember that the darkness of night precedes the dawn. And as long as your heart still beats, this is not the death of it. You don't have to die here.

Sometimes, the ocean floor is only a stop on the journey. And it is when you are at this lowest point, that you are faced with a choice. You can stay there at the bottom, until you drown. Or you can gather pearls and rise again—stronger from the swim, and richer from the jewels.

The only path to God is submission.

'Knowledge' without submission is arrogance,
and a weapon of Ego.

'Spirituality' without submission is
worship of Self and of the 'spiritual high'.

We live in a world where we want things immediately. But, all around us, Allah teaches us a profound lesson, again and again: everything is a process and takes time.

Allah could have made a baby in a moment, but He designed it to take nine months. A seed could have become a massive Oak in a day, but He designed it to take hundreds of years. The Prophet's mission could have been completed in a year or two. But, God designed it to take twenty three.

You will not always see the fruits of your labor right away. Maybe not even in your lifetime. But don't get discouraged. All things take time. And for everything there is a process you cannot speed up. Therefore, success is dependent upon patience (see Quran 3:200).

Hijab is not for angels. Hijab is for flawed, beautiful humans, who are saying every day that they are trying.

And there is so much beauty in that struggle. God sees it. Never belittle any act of love and worship. It could be this act of obedience that God accepts. And it could be because of it, that God forgives your other flaws.

To all those broken or hopeless, I have learned this:

Be grateful for every single person who was part of your story. The ones that hurt you. The ones that helped you. The ones that came, and the ones that left.

They all taught you.

Don't think for a moment that any of it was random. There are no oversights with God. Only perfectly crafted chapters in each unique journey.

To find out more about Yasmin Mogahed and her other writings and events:

BOOKS

Reclaim Your Heart: Personal insights on breaking free from life's shackles   New Edition

SOCIAL MEDIA

Facebook: https://www.facebook.com/YMogahed/

Twitter URL and Handle:
https://twitter.com/YasminMogahed , @YasminMogahed

Website: http://www.yasminmogahed.com/

Instagram: https://www.instagram.com/yasminmogahed/?hl=en

YouTube Channel:
https://www.youtube.com/user/YasminMogahedOnline